THE SEA
IS
BEAUTIFUL
TO ME

9 781300 478423

I0692367

Book Introduction

Welcome to "The Sea is Beautiful to Me," a poetic journey through the wonders and majesty of the ocean. This collection of verses captures the serenity, power, tranquility, and timeless beauty of the sea. Each line is crafted to evoke the sensory experiences of ocean life, from the gentle lapping of waves to the awe-inspiring sight of dramatic cliffs and foggy shores.

Whether you find solace in the rhythmic whispers of the tides, the thrill of exploring the depths, or the joy of seaside adventures, this book is a tribute to the boundless allure of the ocean. So dive in, let your heart and soul be carried away, and let the beauty of the sea wash over you. Let its tranquility calm your mind, its majesty inspire your spirit, and its wonder awaken your sense of curiosity and awe.

Through a series of poetic vignettes, we will take you on a journey to the ocean's edge, where the boundaries between land and sea blur, and the rhythms of nature soothe the soul. We will explore the ocean's ability to inspire, to heal, and to transform, and we will delve into the ways in which it can awaken our sense of wonder, our sense of awe, and our sense of connection to the world around us.

Follow the author on Instagram: @caleb.larsen.54

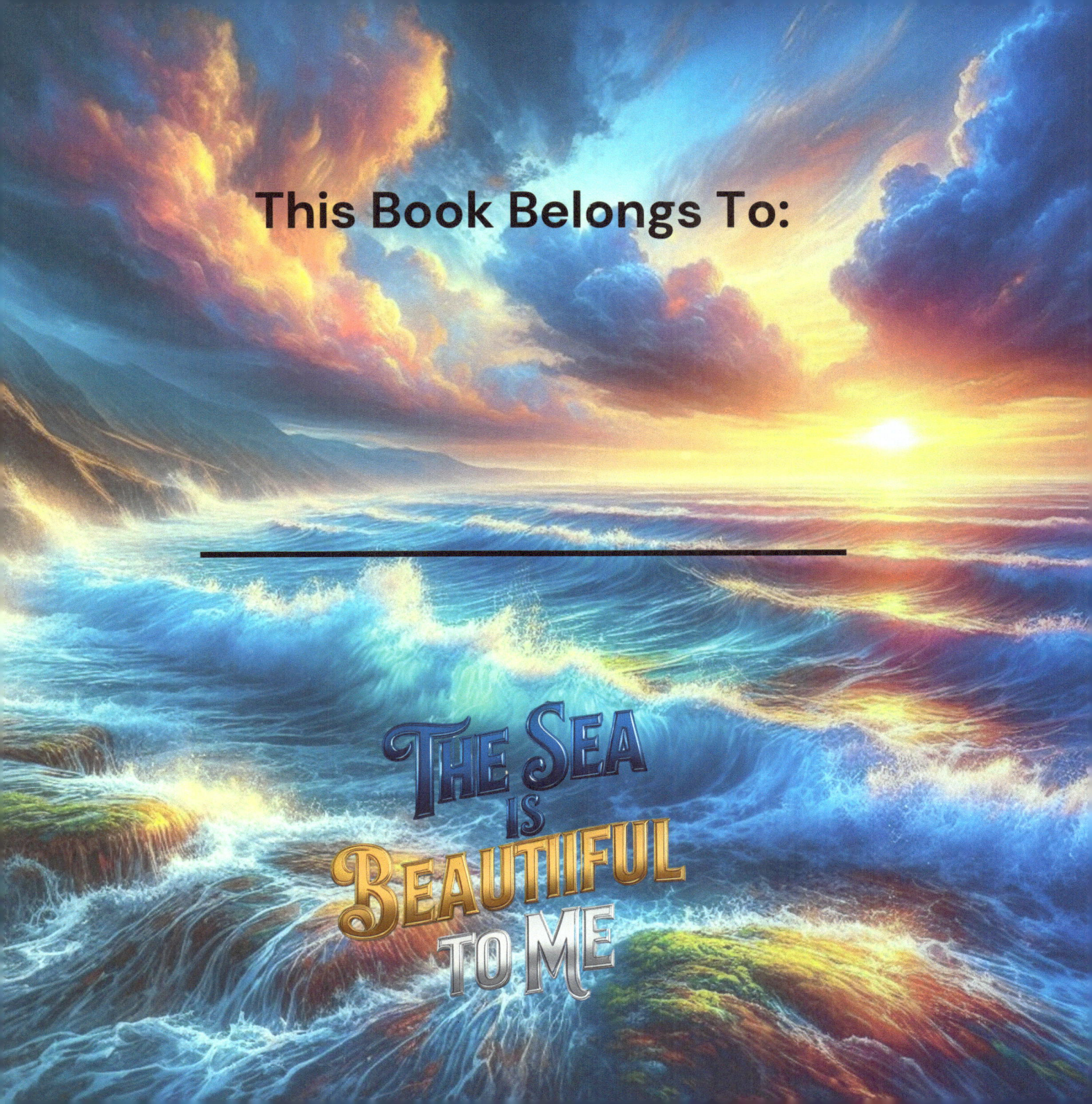

This Book Belongs To:

I love to visit the sea, it's beautiful to me, A place where I find peace, and my heart can be free. The soothing sound of waves crashing against the shore, Echoes the rhythm of my soul, forever more.

The feeling of wet sand between my toes as I walk barefoot on the beach, Is a sensation that grounds me and makes my heart speak. Watching stunning sunrises and sunsets, nature's grand array, Is a reminder of the beauty that's always on display.

The ocean's vastness and open horizon, awe-inspiring and grand, Makes me feel small yet connected to this wondrous land. The cool, salty air of the ocean breeze, refreshing and sweet, Invigorates my senses and makes me feel alive in this enchanted retreat.

From tiny plankton to blue whales, a world of wonder and strife, The ocean is home to an incredible array of life. Exploring the depths, a thrilling dive into the ocean's heart, Riding the waves on a surfboard, thrills that set my soul apart.

Sailing on the ocean can be a calming and enjoyable ride, With stunning views of the coastline and vibrant coral reefs side by side. The ocean has a calming effect on my mind and soul, And offers a sense of freedom and adventure that makes me whole.

With each wave's gentle whisper, the shoreline yields its treasures rare, Shells, sea glass, and secrets, hidden with care. In tidal pools, a microcosm of the ocean's grand design, Creatures thrive and flourish, in a world of wonder, all divine.

The smell of the ocean air is distinctive and invigorating, too, With a hint of salt and seaweed, refreshing and true. The ocean's cool water splashing on my skin, A sense of freedom that awakens from within.

Swimming in the open ocean, a sense of freedom that can't be beat, Renews my spirit, refreshed in the summer heat. Seagulls soaring above in the sky so fair, Their graceful flight a dance with the ocean air.

A romantic walk on the beach, a special chance to align, With nature's beauty and each other, a love that's divine. Spotting dolphins and whales in their natural domain, A thrilling wonder and adventure, a sight that will sustain.

Fascinating shipwrecks offer a glimpse into history and the ocean's might, Unveiling tales of the past, where ship and sea unite. The gentle sway of a hammock by the sea, a calming embrace, A moment to unwind, feeling the ocean's grace.

Visiting coastal towns with history rich and culture so rare, Cobblestone streets and stories fill the air. Each town's unique charm, a tapestry of the past, Echoes of sailors' tales, where memories are vast.

Escape from daily life, no moments of unrest, We find ourselves relaxed, we lay our heads to rest. Meditation, quiet, yoga, and upon the beach we play, Leaving behind the tension, we find peace each day.

A sight to see, nature's raw power firsthand, Watching an ocean storm from a safe distance, exhilarating and grand. Gathering around a beach bonfire, warm and bright, A special experience, a delight in the night.

The ocean makes us feel connected to nature and the world around, Offering a sense of awe, wonder, and appreciation for the beauty and power unbound. Seawater is rich in minerals with properties to renew, Making it popular for healing treatments, refreshing and true.

The ocean's vastness and power, awe-inspiring and grand, With waves, tides, and coastlines, nature's perfect hand. A reminder of beauty and might in endless view, The beach offers fun activities, always something new.

From building sandcastles to kites in flight, Playing volleyball and swimming, such pure delight. A way to enjoy and excite, with endless thrill, The ocean's call, a joy we always feel.

The ocean is a favored spot for romantic escapes, With beaches so beautiful, like celestial capes. Coastal towns with charm, where history meets the sea, A place to unwind, explore, and simply be free.

The ocean's cliffs and rocky coastlines, magnificent and vast, Shrouded in mist, where foggy shores contrast. Breathtaking views, nature's powerful hand, A reminder of its might, so beautiful, so grand.

A sense of vulnerability, where land meets sea, Nature's raw power, wild and free. Dramatic cliffs rise tall, a sight we can't ignore, The ocean's majesty, continues forevermore.

Adventure and possibility thrive in the ocean's embrace, With opportunities for exploration, discovery, and grace. Excitement to live, a way to be free, To see the world, and always be.

I love to visit the sea, it's beautiful to me, A place where I find peace, and my heart can be free, Wild and carefree, in this vast and endless blue, A sanctuary where dreams come true.

Beautiful to me, the sea I love to visit, Where my heart finds its home, in waves so exquisite. In the sea's embrace, my soul is free, I love to visit the sea, it's beautiful to me.

Dear Reader,

As you close this book, I want to take a moment to thank you for floating on this poetic voyage to the ocean's edge. It has been a privilege to share my love for the sea with you, and I hope that these poems have inspired you to appreciate the beauty, wonder, and majesty of the ocean in a new and deeper way.

I hope that you have found solace in the soothing sound of the waves, inspiration in the ocean's majesty, and wonder in its depths. I hope that you have been reminded of the importance of preserving our ocean's beauty and wonder for future generations, and that you have been inspired to take action to protect this precious resource. I hope that the verses have resonated with you, evoking a sense of tranquility and wonder that the ocean so beautifully bestows. May the words inspire you to explore, cherish, and protect the natural world around us. Your connection to the sea is vital to its future.

Most of all, I hope that you have been touched by the beauty of the sea, and that you will carry its wonder and awe with you long after you finish reading this book. Thank you again for joining me on this journey, and I wish you all the best on your own path of discovery and wonder. As always, thank you for reading!

THE SEA IS BEAUTIFUL TO ME

IT'S BEAUTFUL TO ME!

If your heart is big, you know where to begin, Let's help to keep the water clean, let's do our part and win.

Oceans, rivers, lakes, and streams, all need our tender care, Each drop is precious, a treasure we must share.

Give to love and love to protect, The beauty of our planet, let's not neglect.

Picking up litter, reducing waste, For a cleaner Earth, let's act with haste.

Join the cause, spread the word, Protect our waters, let our voices be heard.

From plastic-free shores to pristine blue, A cleaner world starts with me and you.

So open your heart and take a stand, Together we can protect this land.

Let's cherish every waterway, from the smallest pond to the bay, Because I love to visit the sea, it's beautiful to me.